CW01082798

Original title:

The Colors of Me

Copyright © 2024 Creative Arts Management OÜ

All rights reserved.

Author: Alexander Thornton

ISBN HARDBACK: 978-9916-88-872-8

ISBN PAPERBACK: 978-9916-88-873-5

Radiant Reverie

In the dawn's soft, golden glow,
Dreams awaken, gentle and slow.
Whispers of hope in the air,
Life's wonders, beyond compare.

Flowers bloom with colors bright,
Dancing softly in the light.
Every petal tells a tale,
Of the heart that will not fail.

Waves of laughter paint the sky,
As the birds begin to fly.
In this moment, time stands still,
A canvas touched by our will.

Stars will shine, the moon will rise,
Guiding dreams with silver ties.
In our hearts, the magic glows,
Radiant reverie, love grows.

Celestial Palette

Stars like gems in velvet skies,
Whispers of the night arise.
Moonlight spills on quiet streams,
Painting softly all our dreams.

Auroras dance in mystic waves,
Colorful tales the cosmos craves.
Galaxies twirl in cosmic flow,
Crafting shades we long to know.

Living Through Luminous Hues

Every sunrise paints anew,
Brush of gold, a vibrant hue.
Fields of flowers, vivid sights,
Nature's canvas, pure delights.

In the twilight, colors blend,
Shadows stretch as day must end.
Echoes of the day remain,
Living through each bright refrain.

Deep Dives into Vivid Waters

Beneath the waves, a world unfolds,
Coral castles, treasures untold.
Fishes dart like living art,
Diving deep, we play our part.

Rippling light, a gentle sway,
Mysteries in blue display.
As we plunge into the deep,
Vibrancy in silence keep.

Breathing in Vibrance

In the garden, colors sing,
Life awakens with the spring.
Petals soft and fragrances sweet,
Every heartbeat, joy does greet.

Seasons change, yet beauty stays,
Filling our lives in endless ways.
Breathing in each vibrant view,
Finding peace in every hue.

Touched by Spectrum

Bright colors kiss the dawn's light,
Whispers of hues take to flight.
Every shade dances in the breeze,
Painting dreams with perfect ease.

The sun dips low, a golden sphere,
Soft layers shimmer, crystal clear.
In twilight's glow, shadows play,
A vibrant world fades to gray.

Within the Spectrum of Self

Layers of color, deep and bright,
Reflect my journey, day and night.
In every shade, my heart reveals,
The truth within, the soul it heals.

Joy and sorrow intertwine,
In painted strokes, a life divine.
Each hue a chapter, bold and true,
A spectrum wide, the self in view.

Merging in Pastels

Soft pastels blend with ease,
Gentle strokes, a tender breeze.
Whispered colors, sweet and light,
Creating peace in day and night.

Crayons whispered dreams on paper,
Pastel skies, the heart's eraser.
In each swirl a story told,
Merging hues, a sight to behold.

The Dance of Tones

In every note, a world alive,
Colors swirl as tones arrive.
Rhythms pulse beneath the skin,
A vibrant dance where dreams begin.

With every sway, the canvas breathes,
A symphony of life it weaves.
Spiraling into shades unknown,
Together, we find our tone.

Varnished Dreams

In twilight's glow, we chase our light,
Whispers of hope in the quiet night.
With every stroke, our dreams take flight,
Varnished futures, radiant and bright.

Shadows linger, cloaked in mystery,
Each shimmering thought a hidden history.
Together we weave, with threads so fine,
In the tapestry of time, our hearts entwine.

Dappled Desires

Beneath the trees, where sunlight plays,
Dappled desires emerge in rays.
Moments captured in a fleeting glance,
Life's sweet rhythm a gentle dance.

We gather dreams like fallen leaves,
Whispers of laughter the heart believes.
These fleeting thoughts, like birds in flight,
Guide us softly into the night.

Portrait of My Spirit

Canvas stretching, colors collide,
Each brushstroke tells what I can't hide.
In every hue, my essence shines,
A portrait of spirit, where heart aligns.

Through ebbs and flows, I search for grace,
Finding solace in this sacred space.
With every curve, my tale unfolds,
A masterpiece crafted, vibrant and bold.

The Artistry of Being

In every heartbeat, a rhythm divine,
The artistry of being is a sacred design.
With open eyes, we embrace the now,
In each fleeting moment, we take our vow.

Layers unfold like petals in spring,
Celebrating the joy that true life can bring.
In the dance of existence, we find our way,
Crafting our story, day by day.

Radiance of Thought

In the quiet of the mind, light grows,
Illuminating paths where wisdom flows.
Whispers of ideas dance and entwine,
Creating a brilliance, both sharp and divine.

Moments of clarity, profound and true,
Spark inspiration, the old and the new.
Like dawn breaking, dispelling dark night,
The radiance of thought, a guiding light.

Brush with Existence

Each breath a stroke on life's vast canvas,
Coloring moments, both joyous and anxious.
Life's palette rich, in hues we choose,
A masterpiece formed, for win or lose.

We paint our days with laughter and tears,
Sketching our hopes, confronting deep fears.
With every brush, a story unfolds,
In our hands, existence gracefully molds.

Exploring the Depths of Tint

In shades of twilight, mysteries call,
Diving deep within, we risk it all.
Every tint a tale, every hue a key,
Unlocking the secrets of what we can be.

From subtle pastels to vibrant stains,
Life's depth unfurls, joy mixed with pains.
Exploration leads to colors anew,
In every stroke, a journey pursued.

The Vibrancy Within

Beneath the surface, a glow resides,
A symphony of colors that never hides.
Awakening dreams in radiant splendor,
The vibrancy within, a sweet surrender.

With every heartbeat, a canvas we mold,
Stories painted in shades bright and bold.
Letting our spirits dance and flow,
The vibrancy within, forever aglow.

Prism Within

A light breaks through the glass,
Colors dance, a vibrant show.
Each hue tells a story bold,
Whispers secrets only they know.

In the shadows, darkness waits,
Fragments of a hidden truth.
A spark ignites, the soul elates,
Like the joy of distant youth.

Through the spectrum, shadows blend,
In chaos, harmony finds form.
A journey starts, no need to pretend,
In the tempest, the heart stays warm.

Within the prism, worlds collide,
Outside, a wonder ever flows.
Let the colors be your guide,
To where the spirit freely goes.

Shades of Reflection

In quiet waters, thoughts arise,
Mirrored images softly speak.
Shades of lessons hidden deep,
In the silence, I find my peak.

Colors shift at twilight's call,
Mellow indigo, golden light.
Reflections blur, yet stand so tall,
In this moment, all feels right.

Layers peel beneath the gaze,
Each shade a chapter in the past.
In the stillness, wisdom stays,
Through the colors, I hold fast.

Boundless hues of what's to be,
Embracing change, I let it flow.
In these shades, I learn to see,
The beauty in what I know.

Rainbow of Thoughts

In the clouds of my mind's eye,
Thoughts entwine like silver threads.
Each color shines, the dreams soar high,
Whispers of hope fill up my head.

Crimson passion, azure skies,
Violet dreams, and emerald pride.
In this spectrum, freedom flies,
A tapestry, where fears subside.

Through storms and sun, the rain will fall,
Creating arcs of endless grace.
With every stroke, I hear the call,
Of vibrant life in this embrace.

In the corners of my heart,
The rainbow forms a sacred space.
A blend of beauty, a work of art,
In every thought, I find my place.

Tints of My Truth

A canvas waits, a heart exposed,
Daring strokes to paint my soul.
With every hue, a story composed,
In the colors, I become whole.

Tints of joy and shades of pain,
Each stroke tells where I have been.
Through the storms and through the rain,
In this palette, strength is seen.

Each line a journey, bold yet soft,
Every blend a choice to make.
Laughter dances, and sorrows loft,
In the brushstrokes, I awake.

With every layer, I reveal,
The truths that shimmer, spark, and glow.
In these tints, I find what's real,
A masterpiece in ebb and flow.

Vivid Whispers

In shadows where colors blend,
Thoughts ripple like a gentle wind.
Whispers dance through open air,
Tales of love and hearts laid bare.

Dreams awaken with soft light,
Inviting stars to join the night.
Voices murmur, souls unite,
Painting life in hues so bright.

Each moment a brushstroke fine,
Crafting paths through fate's design.
Whispers cloak the fear of change,
Embrace the strange and the mundane.

In the silence, secrets thrive,
Vivid whispers keep hope alive.
Through the canvas of our days,
Life's rich tapestry displays.

Chroma of Experience

Life spills colors on the floor,
Every step brings something more.
In the rush of day-to-day,
Chroma shifts and lights the way.

Moments captured, vivid, clear,
Echoes of joy, tinged with fear.
Brushes dipped in laughter's hue,
Yet shadows paint what we go through.

Through the laughter and the tears,
Each experience builds the years.
Every trial a vibrant shade,
In the heart's gallery arrayed.

Layers deep, we learn to see,
The beauty in our history.
Chroma gleams, a spectrum wide,
In life's dance, we learn to glide.

Tapestry of Feelings

In the loom of heart and mind,
Threads of passion intertwined.
Each emotion, a vibrant strand,
Weaving stories, hand in hand.

Joy and sorrow, laughter's tune,
Fraying edges under the moon.
Textures rich, sensations blend,
Tapestries that never end.

Every whisper holds a tale,
In this fabric, love prevails.
From the darkest threads arise,
Moments that ignite the skies.

Stitched together, we define,
A tapestry, uniquely mine.
Feelings dance in vivid flow,
Crafting life, and love we sow.

Canvas of Self

Blank and open, stretches wide,
A canvas where the dreams reside.
Brush in hand, the heart will guide,
Colors mixed, where hopes abide.

Every stroke ignites the fire,
Creating worlds that we desire.
Shadows form a silent grace,
Reflecting love's warm embrace.

Layers add depth to the day,
Truth revealed in bold display.
In the chaos, we find peace,
A canvas where the fears release.

Shapes emerge, the soul's own art,
A masterpiece that speaks of heart.
With every hue, we tell our fate,
In this canvas, we create.

A Mosaic of Heartbeats

In the silence, whispers stir,
Fragments of dreams softly blur.
Every thump, a story told,
In vibrant hues, our tales unfold.

Each heartbeat paints the night,
Colors swirling in the light.
To the rhythm of love's embrace,
We find our own sacred space.

Moments stitched, a quilt of time,
In every pulse, a reason, a rhyme.
Together we dance through the fray,
Crafting memories day by day.

A canvas bright, emotions shine,
Threads of hope, a life divine.
In each echo, we take part,
Creating a mosaic of heart.

Harmonies in Different Shades

Soft melodies weave the air,
Notes of joy, rhythms rare.
In shadows, colors intertwine,
Harmonies rise, hearts align.

Every tone a gentle sway,
Whispers soft, guiding the way.
In the dance of dusk and dawn,
Life's symphony plays on and on.

Vibrant chords, subtle and sweet,
Every pulse echoes, a heartbeat.
Together, differences blend,
Creating magic, never to end.

In this tapestry we share,
Different shades, a love laid bare.
United by songs softly sung,
In every heart, we are young.

Chromatic Whirlwind

Colors whirl in a vibrant spree,
Spirals move, wild and free.
Every hue a story bright,
In the chaos, finds its light.

Swiftly dancing through the air,
A kaleidoscope, bold and rare.
In the rush, we find our place,
In the whirlwind, a sweet embrace.

Twirling thoughts, a vivid chase,
In every twist, we find grace.
Together swirling, hand in hand,
In this chromatic wonderland.

Life's a canvas, bold and grand,
Every stroke, we understand.
In the whirlwind, love ignites,
Creating joy on starry nights.

Tints of Time

Time flows like a gentle stream,
Carrying whispers of a dream.
Each moment, softly it gleams,
Painting life in vibrant themes.

Golden sunsets, twilight's sigh,
Memories linger as they fly.
In the hues of dusk and dawn,
We cherish what we've drawn.

A palette rich with hopes and fears,
Captured laughter, fallen tears.
Every tint a flicker bright,
Guiding us through day and night.

As we journey through this space,
Time's embrace, a warm embrace.
In the tints, we rise and fall,
Finding beauty in it all.

Chromatic Adventures

Colors swirl in vibrant hues,
Bringing life to thoughts we choose.
With each shade, a story spins,
In the light, our journey begins.

Fields of green and skies so blue,
Whispers of the world feel new.
Every shade a different song,
In this dance, we all belong.

Brush of red, a flame ensues,
Golden rays like morning dew.
Exploring realms both far and wide,
With every color, fears subside.

In the spectrum, we will find,
A tapestry of heart and mind.
Chromatic dreams, let's set them free,
In this adventure, you and me.

Radiant Ruminations

Thoughts like sunbeams break the dawn,
In the quiet, hopes are drawn.
Reflecting on the day's embrace,
Every moment, a sacred space.

Images of joy and pain,
In the stillness, wisdom reigns.
Radiant truths begin to glow,
In the depths where dreams do flow.

Silent musings in the night,
Stars above, a guiding light.
In the shadows, fears take flight,
Embracing all that feels so right.

From the heart, the echoes sound,
In our thoughts, freedom is found.
Radiant ruminations flow,
In the light, our spirits grow.

Variegated Journeys

Paths unfold in myriad ways,
Winding through both sunlit days.
Every twist a lesson learned,
In the heart, a fire burned.

Across the hills and through the trees,
With the winds, we ride the breeze.
Varied landscapes, stories blend,
With each step, new horizons bend.

Journeys painted with great care,
Every moment, the world to share.
In the colors of the sky,
We discover how, and why.

Hand in hand, we wander wide,
Side by side, with hearts as guides.
Variegated journeys lead,
To the dreams we all will heed.

Luminous Layers

Beneath the surface, light resides,
In hidden depths, our soul confides.
Each layer reveals what's inside,
In the darkness, dreams abide.

Luminous glimmers, soft and bright,
Breaking through the cloak of night.
In shadows cast, our thoughts arise,
With every glimmer, knowledge flies.

Peeling back the veil of fears,
Finding strength through silent tears.
In the layers, truths await,
Guiding us to our own fate.

Let the light embrace your heart,
In every layer, play your part.
Luminous paths shall lead us near,
To the wisdom we hold dear.

Dancing with Tints

Colors swirl in a playful breeze,
Whispers of joy, they aim to please.
In the twilight, shadows blend,
A canvas where dreams ascend.

Each hue dances, a vibrant song,
Crafting stories where we belong.
With every step, the shades embrace,
A harmonious waltz, a timeless grace.

Luminescence of Existence

In the dark, a flicker glows,
Life ignites, and wonder flows.
Stars above, a guiding light,
Illuminating paths so bright.

Each heartbeat sings, a radiant tune,
In the vastness, we are strewn.
Moments shimmer, a sacred dance,
In existence, we find our chance.

Palette of the Past

Brush strokes of memories untold,
Fragments of youth, both brave and bold.
Echoes of laughter in distant skies,
Where innocence and time comply.

Colors fade, yet still remain,
Each tale woven, mingled with pain.
A tapestry worn, but rich in hue,
The past's embrace, forever true.

The Glow of My Essence

Within my core, a fire ignites,
A gentle warmth, a million lights.
In silence, my spirit sings,
Crafting solace that life brings.

With every breath, I shine and sway,
Reflecting beauty in my own way.
A light that bends, yet stands so tall,
The glow of my essence, embracing all.

Hues Woven in Silence

In the quiet twilight glow,
Whispers paint the sky,
Soft shades of deep indigo,
As night begins to sigh.

Crimson blends with velvet blue,
In a dance, they sway,
Merging dreams that hush anew,
In the fading day.

The stars emerge, a silver thread,
Stitched in cosmic grace,
While shadows drift and softly spread,
In this tranquil space.

A canvas brushed by gentle hands,
With secrets held so tight,
In hues where silence makes its stands,
A world of pure delight.

Tints of Laughter

In a field where sunflowers grin,
Joy spills in bursts of gold,
Every petal, stories spin,
Of laughter yet untold.

Rainbow arcs cross azure skies,
Chasing clouds of white,
With every giggle, summer flies,
In warmth of sheer delight.

The breeze carries a playful tune,
Soft notes of childhood play,
Fleeting moments, afternoons,
In the bright ballet.

With every step, the colors burst,
In vibrant, swirling dance,
Embraced by joy, we quench our thirst,
In laughter's sweet expanse.

Colorful Echoes of Tomorrow

Brush the dawn with rays of light,
In shades of soft embrace,
Each hue a promise, fresh and bright,
Of dreams we dare to chase.

The canvas waits for strokes of hope,
With every dawn anew,
A kaleidoscope, we learn to cope,
In colors bold and true.

Through misty trails of emerald green,
Paths of potential gleam,
In echoes of what might have been,
We weave our waking dream.

As shadows fade, let colors soar,
In every heartbeat's song,
A tapestry of evermore,
Where we all belong.

A Symphony of Shades

In the twilight's gentle hand,
Shadows paint the evening red,
With every brush, a note we stand,
In colors softly spread.

The blues of dusk, deep and alluring,
Whisper secrets, old and wise,
Through their tones, the heart's enduring,
Crafting dreams beneath the skies.

Golden tones of laughter rise,
As daylight bids adieu,
In harmony where silence lies,
And echoes come in view.

A symphony that swells and bends,
With every shade, a part,
In this world where beauty blends,
And colors speak to heart.

Reflections in Every Hue.

In the mirror, colors blend,
Whispers of a life, they send.
Shadows dance in shades of gray,
Every hue has come to play.

Silent moments, soft and bright,
Past reflections, shared at night.
Blues of sorrow, reds of fire,
Every tone ignites desire.

In the dawn, a gentle glow,
Golden rays begin to flow.
Whirling colors in the sky,
Paint my dreams as they go by.

At twilight's end, the colors fade,
Yet in my heart, they won't evade.
Each reflection tells my truth,
In every shade, I find my youth.

Spectrum of My Soul

In the spectrum, see me shine,
Each day brings a twist divine.
From sweet pastels to deep, dark hues,
Every color shares my views.

Greens of hope and purest joy,
Tints of laughter none can destroy.
In every shade, a story told,
Colors shifting, fierce and bold.

In the silence, colors clash,
Passions burn, emotions flash.
Violet dreams and azure skies,
Every shade, a spark that flies.

As the light begins to wane,
Find my truth amidst the pain.
In this dance of light and shade,
Spectrum of my soul displayed.

Palette of Emotions

With every stroke, my heart unfolds,
An artist's brush, my story told.
Bright yellows sing of sunny days,
While shadows lurk in muted grays.

Crimson love and emerald pride,
In this canvas, I confide.
Turquoise tears and sapphire dreams,
Life's palette, bursting at the seams.

With every drip, the canvas breathes,
Joy and sorrow, intertwined leaves.
A vivid mess, yet beautiful too,
Each emotion paints a different view.

As the masterpiece comes alive,
Understanding how I thrive.
In every color, I find my way,
A palette of emotions at play.

Hues of Identity

In my heart, a spectrum flows,
Colors shifting, only I know.
Each hue tells of where I've been,
A journey in the skin I've seen.

Ivory whispers and onyx screams,
Mauve memories, childhood dreams.
Chartreuse laughter, deep indigo pain,
Every shade carved from the rain.

Melded identities intertwine,
In every shade, a life's design.
Carved with love, shaped by the past,
These hues of me will ever last.

As I navigate this vibrant show,
Embracing all the highs and lows.
In every color, I see my pride,
Hues of identity, none can hide.

Shades of Transformation

In twilight's glow, the shadows dance,
Whispers of change in a fleeting glance.
Colors blend, as daylight fades,
Embracing night, as magic pervades.

A butterfly sheds its weary skin,
Emerging anew, let the journey begin.
Each layer falls, revealing light,
In the soft hush of a starry night.

With every breath, a shift occurs,
Breaking the silence, nature stirs.
In the cycle of life, truths unfold,
Like stories whispered, waiting to be told.

So here I stand, amidst the hues,
Caught in the currents of shifting views.
From dark to light, I take my place,
In shades of transformation, I find grace.

Unfolding My Canvas

With a brush of dreams, I start to paint,
Every stroke a whisper, a hesitant saint.
Colors collide on a blank expanse,
Unfolding my canvas, a visual dance.

Each corner holds a different tale,
Of joy and sorrow, the winds that sail.
Textures rise with a gentle sigh,
In the silence of hours, my spirit flies.

Dappled sunsets and morning dew,
A splash of laughter, a hint of blue.
Lines intertwine, bold and shy,
Filling the void where thoughts can tie.

In the chaos, I find my voice,
In swirls of color, I make my choice.
This canvas reflects the heart's decree,
Unfolding my journey, wild and free.

Whirls of Imagination

In dreams, the spirals spin and glide,
Moments captured, where fantasies reside.
Each thought a petal, a whimsical flight,
In whirls of imagination, day turns to night.

A tapestry woven with visions bright,
Creativity dances, igniting the light.
Stars flicker softly in shadows cast,
Innovations blossom, a bridge to the past.

Through the nebulous clouds, ideas soar,
Inviting the heart to explore once more.
With each breath, a new story unfolds,
Whirls of imagination, infinite golds.

So let us dream with eyes wide open,
With every heartbeat, our spirits awoken.
In a universe vast, let our thoughts play,
Whirls of imagination guide our way.

Embracing the Spectrum

Light refracts through prisms of grace,
Creating colors that time can't erase.
In every hue, a story is spun,
Embracing the spectrum, we become one.

From crimson reds to calming blues,
Each shade whispers secrets, a chance to choose.
Bright yellows emerge, warming the day,
In the dance of colors, we find our way.

The gentle greens breathe life anew,
While violets remind us of dreams in view.
Textures mingle, and feelings entwine,
In this vibrant tapestry, hearts align.

So let us gather in this radiant light,
Celebrating differences, shining so bright.
United in hues, together we sing,
Embracing the spectrum, love is our spring.

Identity in Vivid Brushstrokes

In a canvas splashed with dreams,
My essence flows like streams.
Colors collide in bold embrace,
Whispers of my storied grace.

Each hue a piece of me,
Tales of love and history.
Splattered thoughts, bright and clear,
Striking chords that all can hear.

Underneath the vibrant shade,
Layers of my truth displayed.
A mosaic of every fight,
Crafted with a fearless light.

In this art, my soul is seen,
Boundless as the sky's pure sheen.
Every stroke, a heartfelt claim,
In vivid colors, I find my name.

Vibrant Echoes

Whispers dance in colors bold,
Stories of the brave, untold.
Each echo carries weight and sound,
A symphony of lives profound.

In the mirror, I can trace,
Reflections of a countless face.
Colors blend, yet stand apart,
Crafting rhythms of the heart.

Through the spectrum, I perceive,
Endless dreams we all believe.
In every shade, a life unfolds,
Vibrant echoes never cold.

So let us sing in hues so bright,
Unite the shadows, bring the light.
Together we can paint the dawn,
In vibrant echoes, we belong.

My Multicolored Essence

In every color chosen true,
Lies a piece of me and you.
My life, a tapestry of grace,
Woven in this sacred space.

Bold reds pulse with love's sweet fire,
Gentle greens in nature's choir.
Each shade tells a secret tale,
Of storms endured, yet bright sails.

Yellows burst like laughter's song,
Blues embrace where hearts belong.
With every brush, I claim my ground,
In multicolored essence found.

From shadows cast to light embraced,
I celebrate the path I've traced.
In each stroke, my spirit flies,
A vibrant soul in painted skies.

Harmonizing the Hues

In symphony of shades I dwell,
A harmony that words can't tell.
Each color sings its unique tune,
Together in a vibrant swoon.

Oranges glow like sunsets bright,
Purples whisper in the night.
Through this palette, hearts unite,
Creating visions pure and right.

As we blend, our stories merge,
A canvas born from life's great surge.
In every hue, connection grows,
A masterpiece that ever flows.

Together we arise and soar,
In harmony, we find much more.
With each color, fresh and bold,
We sing of life in strokes untold.

The Essence of My Being

In the stillness of the night,
I seek the core of me,
A flicker in the dark,
Where shadows long to be.

Cascading thoughts like rivers,
Flowing through my mind,
I gather every whisper,
Of dreams intertwined.

With every breath I take,
I sense the pulse of life,
The essence of my being,
Beyond the joy and strife.

A tapestry of moments,
Woven with my heart,
Each thread a silent story,
A masterpiece of art.

Colors in the Silence

In quietude, I linger,
Where colors softly play,
A canvas rich and vibrant,
In whispers of the day.

Shades of blue and amber,
Dance within my sight,
Each hue a gentle secret,
Wrapped in the soft light.

The silence sings in rainbows,
Every pulse, a tune,
A symphony of stillness,
Beneath the silver moon.

In the heart of silence,
I find a world anew,
Where colors blend and mingle,
Creating skies of blue.

Whispers of Brightness

Golden rays of morning,
Greet my wandering eyes,
Whispers of brightness call me,
To dance beneath the skies.

In fields of swaying daisies,
The laughter of the leaves,
Each gentle breeze that brushes,
A tale that nature weaves.

Bright thoughts like fireflies,
Illuminate the night,
With every spark of wonder,
I embrace pure delight.

The world is woven softly,
With threads of shining light,
In whispers of brightness,
My spirit takes to flight.

Melodies in Every Hue

In every shade of sunset,
A melody unfolds,
Each color softly singing,
A story to be told.

The crimson notes of passion,
Blend gently with the gold,
Creating harmonies,
Through moments brave and bold.

In twilight's calm embrace,
I hear the hues collide,
A symphony of colors,
Where dreams and hopes abide.

With every brush of twilight,
The world begins to bloom,
In melodies of every hue,
A heart that finds its room.

Echoes in Every Shade

Whispers drift in twilight's gleam,
Colors blend, like a fading dream.
Moments wrapped in soft embrace,
Time reveals its gentle face.

Steps echo on the empty street,
Where shadows and memories meet.
Each laugh and sigh, a gentle trace,
Paints the night with silent grace.

Fading light through branches high,
Streaks of gold in the evening sky.
Nature hums a soothing tune,
As stars emerge like a silver boon.

In every hue, a story told,
Life's tapestry, both warm and cold.
Echoes dance, forever played,
A symphony in every shade.

Melodies in Various Tones

Each note flows like a gentle stream,
Carrying whispers of a dream.
Rhythms pulse in the evening air,
A song that lingers everywhere.

From soft piano to trumpet's call,
Music rises, then begins to fall.
Harmony weaves through every lane,
Crafted from joy, from love, from pain.

Voices blend in the dusky light,
Creating magic, pure and bright.
Every verse tells a tale so bold,
In melodies, life's truths unfold.

In every tune, a heartbeat found,
Resonates in the vibrant sound.
Melodies weave a rich array,
Binding us in a grand ballet.

Palette of Memories

A canvas filled with vibrant hues,
Each splash a fragment of our views.
Brushstrokes rich, both soft and bold,
Stories captured, waiting to be told.

Colors swirl in a dance of light,
Echoes of laughter, shadows of night.
Every shade, a fleeting glance,
Life unfolds in a vivid dance.

Pastels whisper of days gone by,
While bright shades beckon from the sky.
A palette crafted from heartbeats shared,
Each moment cherished, lovingly bared.

In every stroke, a smile, a tear,
Memories painted, forever near.
The canvas breathes, forever free,
A tapestry of you and me.

Chromatic Journeys

Paths unfold in a spectrum wide,
Colors beckon, hearts collide.
Every turn, a new delight,
Journeys crafted by day and night.

Mountains rise from fields of green,
Splashes of gold in spaces between.
Each step taken, a tale begins,
In chromatic worlds where adventure spins.

Through valleys deep and skies so vast,
We chase the moments, holding fast.
With every shade, a path that's true,
Adventures painted, me and you.

In life's rich tapestry, we roam,
A spectrum wide, we call it home.
With colors bright, our spirits soar,
In chromatic journeys, forevermore.

Spectrum of Serendipity

In whispers soft, the colors blend,
A twist of fate, around the bend.
Life dances, sings, in joyful hues,
A tapestry of chance, to choose.

With every step, a spark ignites,
The universe conspires, delights.
In laughter shared, or quiet sighs,
We find the magic in our skies.

Moments linger, sweet and rare,
In serendipity, we dare.
Each stumble leads to paths unknown,
In vibrant places, seeds are sown.

So let us walk, hand in hand,
Through the painted, playful land.
With open hearts, and eyes to see,
The spectrum wide, of destiny.

Vivid Threads of Being

Through the fabric of the day,
Colors weave in bright array.
Echoes of laughter fill the air,
Each moment cherished, none to spare.

In vibrant threads, our stories spin,
We find the places we begin.
Connections made, and lives entwined,
In every heartbeat, love defined.

With every smile, a light ignites,
In vivid dreams, our souls take flight.
Moments shared, both near and far,
Marking journeys, who we are.

So hold these threads, both strong and fine,
Together, let our spirits shine.
In the tapestry we create,
A vibrant world, our shared fate.

Mosaics of Moments

Fragments glimmer, pieces bright,
In every corner, pure delight.
A mosaic born from time and space,
Each shard a memory, a trace.

We gather stories, one by one,
Underneath the warming sun.
In tiny glances, laughter shared,
A life mosaic, deeply cared.

In chaos, order finds its way,
As colors blend, at close of day.
Each moment shapes the heart's design,
Unified, our lives align.

So cherish every tiny piece,
In mosaics, love finds peace.
Together, we create the whole,
In vibrant hues, the heart and soul.

Shades of Stillness

In quietude, the shadows play,
Soft whispers in the light of day.
Amidst the silence, thoughts unfold,
In stillness, secrets softly told.

The hush of night brings gentle dreams,
In silver beams, the moonlight gleams.
With every breath, the world slows down,
In soothing peace, we rest our crowns.

Moments linger, pure and clear,
In shades of stillness, we draw near.
A sanctuary, found within,
Where every loss can be a win.

So let us savor quiet grace,
In stillness, find our sacred space.
For in the calm, our hearts align,
In every shade, the world divine.

Vibrant Inner Landscapes

A garden blooms within my mind,
Colors dance, a joy unconfined.
Thoughts flutter lightly on the breeze,
Whispers of memories among the leaves.

Mountains rise with dreams untold,
Rivers flow with currents bold.
Sunsets paint the skies with grace,
A tranquil heart finds its place.

Pathways twist through shadows cast,
Echoes of the future and past.
In this realm, I roam and play,
Seeking light at the close of day.

Vibrant hues in every phase,
Life, a canvas, ever ablaze.
In my soul, the colors blend,
Awakening, they never end.

Canvas of Identity

Strokes of laughter fill the air,
Lines of sorrow drawn with care.
A patchwork quilt of joys and fears,
Embroidered with forgotten tears.

Each hue reveals a story's birth,
Mapping moments, giving worth.
Echoes linger in every shade,
Tales of love and dreams we've made.

Brushes dipped in shades so real,
Authentic strokes, the heart can feel.
In every crease, the truth will show,
A vibrant life, as we all grow.

This canvas speaks without a sound,
In its embrace, my soul is found.
Every layer, a piece of me,
A journey woven endlessly.

Tints of Time

Seasons change, colors unfold,
Stories whispered, ages hold.
Sunrise paints the dawn anew,
While twilight fades in muted hue.

In memories, the tints remain,
Faded laughter, shadowed pain.
Every moment a brushstroke fine,
Capturing life, the taste of time.

Gentle pastels of yesterday,
Through the years, they softly sway.
In every heartbeat, every sigh,
The canvas stretches, learning to fly.

Time spills colors, rich and deep,
In its embrace, we dream and leap.
With every tick, a tale is spun,
Tints of time weave us as one.

Brushstrokes of Experience

Each brushstroke tells a tale untold,
Wisdom gained and courage bold.
Textures rough, yet smooth in kind,
Layers of life forever entwined.

Moments crafted with intent,
Strokes of joy and calm lament.
Fragments pieced from trials faced,
In the gallery of dreams interlaced.

Chapters written in colors bright,
Guiding us through the darkest night.
With every stroke, a lesson learned,
In the fire of life, the heart has burned.

Emotions flow, raw and sincere,
A masterpiece we hold most dear.
Together our stories rise and soar,
Brushstrokes of experience, forever more.

Tones of Existence

In whispers of dawn, soft hues arise,
Painting the world with gentle sighs.
Each note of life, a melody spun,
In the vast expanse, we all are one.

Life dances lightly, on fragile threads,
Through laughter and tears, where hope treads.
With shadows that linger, and bright, bold lights,
In the tapestry woven, our spirit ignites.

Colors collide, in a tempest of grace,
Transforming the void, in infinite space.
Moments unfurl, like petals in spring,
Unraveling tales that only hearts sing.

So breathe in the tones that swell in the air,
Each heartbeat echoes, a sacred prayer.
In the gallery of time, where memories glow,
We find our existence, in each undertow.

Brushstrokes of Memory

In the canvas of night, stars gently gleam,
Each twinkle a whisper, a forgotten dream.
Brushstrokes of laughter, pain intertwined,
The art of our lives, in colors defined.

Waves of the past, a soft ebb and flow,
Carrying stories that time can't bestow.
With pigments so rich, they swirl and they blend,
In the heart's gallery, where shadows transcend.

Fleeting moments caught in a painter's embrace,
A symphony captured, a tender trace.
Each stroke tells a story that never grows old,
In the silence of memories, our truths unfold.

So we hold the brush, let the stories flow,
Each hue drips with love, in twilight's glow.
In the brushstrokes of memory, we find our way,
Through the vibrant whispers of yesterday.

Colorful Echoes

In laughter of children, colors resound,
Echoes of joy in the small things found.
With splashes of red, and blue's gentle embrace,
The palette of life leaves a radiant trace.

Nature's own chorus sings vibrant and true,
Each echo a message, in every hue.
From verdant greens to the warm golden rays,
Every shade whispers in myriad ways.

The rhythm of seasons paints skies overhead,
As frost turns to bloom, and soft petals spread.
In echoes of change, we learn to adapt,
Through kaleidoscope visions, reality's mapped.

So let the colors dance through the air,
With echoes of laughter, beyond despair.
In the canvas of life, vibrant and bright,
We find our connection, in day and in night.

Pigments of Passion

In the heart's deep chamber, colors ignite,
With pigments of passion, bold and bright.
Each stroke tells a story of love unconfined,
In the art of our souls, true beauty we find.

Whispers of longing, in shades of desire,
Electric embrace, a dance of fire.
Crimson and azure, wild rhythms collide,
In the tapestry woven, where hearts coincide.

Through storms and through sunshine, we flourish and
grow,
Filling the canvas with the truths that we know.
With every heartbeat, a vibrant refrain,
In pigments of passion, we rise from the rain.

So let us paint boldly, with fervor and grace,
The essence of love, in this beautiful space.
In the gallery of life, where dreams come alive,
With pigments of passion, our spirits will thrive.

Light, Shadow, and Everything in Between

In dawn's embrace, warm rays alight,
Casting shadows, a dance of night.
Colors merge, the world ignites,
Whispers of dreams that take their flight.

Between the hue and dark's soft reign,
Lies the balance of joy and pain.
Moments captured, lost, and found,
In silent echoes, they rebound.

The sun above, the moon below,
A cycle endless, a gentle flow.
In twilight's grasp, we find our way,
Through light and shadow, night and day.

So let us wander, hand in hand,
In the puzzle of life, we take our stand.
For every shadow, there's a beam,
Together weaving the fabric of dream.

Portraits of Vivid Moments

Captured smiles in a fleeting gaze,
Laughter echoes through sunlit haze.
Time stands still in vivid hues,
Tales are painted, a life to choose.

Colors blend in joyous swirls,
Moments cherished, a dance of pearls.
In each frame, a story lies,
Reflections of hopes under endless skies.

Underneath the stars, we pause,
In memories bright, we find our cause.
Each fleeting second, a treasure to keep,
Awash in colors, both bold and deep.

So let's create, together as one,
Tapestries woven till day is done.
In vibrant portraits, we find the fight,
A canvas of life, forever bright.

A Dreamscape in Color

In twilight's glow, a dream takes flight,
Colors swirl in the soft twilight.
A canvas vast where whispers blend,
With shades of hope that never end.

Mountains rise in pastel skies,
Seas of gold where silence lies.
In the depth of night, stars softly gleam,
Guiding us through a vivid dream.

Figures dance in the milk-white mist,
Captured in a moment, a painter's twist.
Brushstrokes of courage, freedom's lore,
A world awakened, forevermore.

Here in this realm, let hearts collide,
In colors bright, we'll freely glide.
Together we'll wander, hand in hand,
In a dreamscape colored by our own brand.

Weaving in the Palette of Life

Threads of laughter, colors entwined,
In the loom of life, beauty defined.
Weaving moments, both bright and pale,
Every stitch tells a wondrous tale.

From sorrows deep to joys that soar,
We blend the shades, forever more.
In the tapestry, each knot we tie,
A story of love that will never die.

Life's a canvas, wide and grand,
We paint our dreams with guiding hand.
With every hue, we make our mark,
In shadows bright, we find our spark.

So let us gather, in colors vast,
Creating a future that holds the past.
In the palette of dreams that never fade,
We weave our lives, our own charade.

Surfaces of Reflection

In the stillness, waters gleam,
Mountains echo, whispering dreams.
Beneath the sky, a world unfolds,
Mirrored stories, quietly told.

The moonlight dances, shadows sway,
Cascading light at the end of day.
Ripples speak in gentle tones,
Secrets held in nature's bones.

Gazing deep, we find our selves,
Within each layer, a thousand elves.
Every glance, a new engage,
Reflecting life on every page.

Surfaces dream, layers collide,
In this vastness, we abide.
Nature's canvas ever wide,
In reflections, we confide.

The Spectrum of Heart

Colors blend in passion's fire,
Each hue ignites a fierce desire.
From crimson love to azure calm,
In every shade, there lies a balm.

Yellow laughter, bright and bold,
Green of hope, in stories told.
Shades of sadness, softest grey,
Melodies in colors play.

Hearts entwined in vibrant ties,
Painting dreams beneath the skies.
Each stroke a memory, a part,
Crafted deep within the heart.

The spectrum shifts with every breath,
Life unfolds in shades of death.
In every color, joy and pain,
Together form our sweet refrain.

A Tapestry of Tints

Woven threads of every shade,
In the fabric, worlds are laid.
Every tint a tale unfolds,
Stories whispered, mysteries bold.

In the warp, the weft does dance,
Life's moments in a fleeting glance.
Crimson strands for love and loss,
Golden joys come at a cost.

Patterns shift with every thread,
In a maze where footsteps tread.
Each hue a journey, every weave,
Tapestries that we believe.

From the dark to light's embrace,
In this art, we find our place.
Threads of fate entwined and spun,
A glorious quilt for everyone.

Reflections in Color

In pools of paint, we see our soul,
Each hue a piece that makes us whole.
Blues that echo, reds that call,
Making light of shadows tall.

Underneath the painter's hand,
Vivid tales, both wild and grand.
Sunset oranges blend with night,
In colors deep, we find our light.

Brush strokes tell what words can't say,
In every splash, our fears at bay.
From dark to dawn, a journey bright,
Reflections in the morning light.

In the spectrum, we find our way,
Through colors bold, we dance and sway.
Heartbeats pulse in shades unknown,
In reflections, we call home.

Shades of My Soul

In twilight's glow, I find my peace,
Colors blend, their whispers cease.
Each shade tells tales of joy and pain,
In the silent echoes, love will reign.

A canvas stretched beneath the stars,
With every stroke, I mend my scars.
Soft blues remind me of dreams unchased,
While fiery reds bring passions embraced.

The greens of nature, calm and bright,
Fill my spirit with pure delight.
Yet shadows linger, deep and bold,
In every hue, my story's told.

With brush in hand, I paint my truth,
A vibrant blend of age and youth.
In the palette of life, I find my whole,
Each stroke a secret, shades of my soul.

Palette of a Whisper

A gentle breeze, a soft-spoken sigh,
Carries colors across the sky.
Whispers blend with the hues of dawn,
In every moment, beauty is drawn.

Pinks and golds in a lover's embrace,
Soft pastel tones, a tender trace.
Brush against the world, a fleeting glance,
In every whisper, a chance to dance.

The charcoal gray of thoughts unseen,
Mixes with laughter, a joyful sheen.
I gather silence, let it unfurl,
In the palette of whispers, I twirl.

With every sound that the wind sings,
A palette forms from the smallest things.
Colors collide, a symphonic sweep,
In this artistry, my heart will keep.

Hues of Heartbeats

Racing rhythms in vibrant tones,
Each heartbeat whispers, never alone.
Bright yellows pulse with hope anew,
While deep violets cradle the blue.

The pink of laughter fills the air,
Like petals dancing without a care.
In every thump, in every sigh,
A vivid spectrum, as days fly by.

Greens of envy and azure of dreams,
Blend together like flowing streams.
Every hue tells its own refrain,
A tapestry woven from joy and pain.

In each heartbeat, colors dive,
Echoes of feeling, so alive.
I gather them close, let them unfold,
These hues of heartbeats, stories retold.

Tapestry of Emotions

Thread by thread, my feelings weave,
A tapestry rich, more than you believe.
Golds of happiness sparkle bright,
While silvers shimmer in the night.

Each emotion is a vibrant strand,
Intertwined, together we stand.
Crimson anger, soft teal of peace,
In every clash, a sweet release.

The browns of grounding, the blacks of fear,
Weaving moments that draw us near.
In every twist, in every turn,
Lessons of love and trust we learn.

Life's rich fabric, layered and bold,
Stories of warmth in threads of gold.
In this tapestry, I will find,
The beauty of feelings forever entwined.

Spectrum of Dreams

In the meadow, colors blend,
Whispers of thoughts, on winds they send.
Softly they dance, in twilight's glow,
Painting hopes where wishes flow.

Beneath the stars, stories take flight,
Each dream a spark in the vast night.
Chasing the echoes of laughter bright,
As shadows fade, welcoming light.

From dawn to dusk, they intertwine,
A tapestry woven, hearts align.
In every shade, a tale unfolds,
A journey of life, a treasure of gold.

In silence, they speak, a gentle hum,
Each vibrant thought, a beat of drum.
Together they rise, together they soar,
In the spectrum of dreams, forevermore.

Layers of Light and Shadow

In the quiet dusk, shapes arise,
Darkness whispers, under fading skies.
The dance of light, the flicker of time,
A world unveiled, in rhythm and rhyme.

Fleeting moments, shadows cast,
In gentle embrace, the light is vast.
Each layer speaks of stories old,
In every hue, a truth unfolds.

From bright beginnings to soft goodbyes,
Through the veil of night, a spark still lies.
Mingling together, they softly blend,
In the heart of twilight, dreams ascend.

Reflections linger, a silent muse,
In light and dark, we choose our views.
Through layered worlds, we find our way,
In shadows deep, hope lights the day.

Essence in Every Hue

From crimson dawn to azure blue,
Every spectrum sings, a vibrant view.
Nature's palette, brushed with care,
In every hue, stories bare.

Emerald greens of life so bold,
Golden whispers of tales untold.
Cerulean skies, where dreams ignite,
In every shade, pure delight.

Saffron sunsets, warming the soul,
Violet nights where time is whole.
Each color a dance, a fleeting chance,
Essences weave in a timeless trance.

In every hue, the heart will know,
The language of life in silent flow.
From dusk till dawn, a journey true,
We find our essence in every hue.

Echoes in Vividity

In the valley deep, echoes play,
Colors ring out, brightening the day.
Each sound a splash, in rhythmic delight,
In vivid strokes, the world feels right.

Through whispers soft, the colors call,
Lifting spirits, brightening all.
From laughter's tone to silence vast,
Moments captured, shadows cast.

In vibrant cries, emotions surge,
Life's true canvas, we converge.
As colors echo, hearts align,
In vivid tales, our dreams entwine.

Through every step, the echoes resound,
Creating symphonies, joy abound.
In the dance of life, we find our place,
Echoes in vividness, a warm embrace.

Serenity in Shades

Whispers of the gentle breeze,
Underneath the dancing trees,
Softly painted skies of blue,
In the calm, I find my view.

Rippling water, crystal clear,
Nature's beauty, drawing near,
Moments wrapped in tender grace,
In this peace, I find my place.

Shadows cast by fading light,
Fleeting day turns into night,
Heart at ease, I close my eyes,
Finding solace in the skies.

In the stillness, time stands still,
Every breath, a joyful thrill,
Serenity, my heart's embrace,
In the quiet, I find space.

Emotions in Full Bloom

Fields awaken, colors bright,
Petals dancing in the light,
Joyful laughter fills the air,
In this moment, free from care.

Hearts entwined, a fragrant kiss,
Every heartbeat is pure bliss,
Sorrow fades, replaced by hope,
In love's garden, we can cope.

Memories like blossoms grow,
In the sun's warm, golden glow,
Every tear can bloom anew,
Emotions rich in every hue.

Boundless dreams in colors swirl,
Life's a canvas, let it unfurl,
With every shade, a story told,
In full bloom, our hearts unfold.

A Hued Journey

Every step, a tale untold,
Colors vibrant, brave and bold,
Through the valleys, up the hills,
In every challenge, find the thrills.

Sunrise whispers shades of gold,
In the twilight, purple's hold,
Moments cherished, shadows cast,
A tapestry that holds us fast.

Every turn, a different view,
Painted skies in every hue,
Life's a journey, ever new,
With each step, I grow with you.

Time's embrace, a gentle wave,
With every breath, a world to save,
Colors blend, create our song,
In this journey, we belong.

Canvas of Life

On life's canvas, brush in hand,
Every stroke, a chance to stand,
Moments captured, vibrant scenes,
In the frame of our routines.

Palette rich with laughter, tears,
Brush away the silent fears,
Layered dreams and hopes collide,
In this art, our hearts reside.

Textures woven, bold and fine,
In every corner, love will shine,
Splashes of joy, dabs of pain,
This masterpiece, our hearts contain.

With time's passage, colors fade,
Yet in truth, we're not afraid,
For every canvas bears our name,
In life's art, we stake our claim.

A Symphony in Shades

In twilight's embrace, colors collide,
Soft whispers of gold, where dreams abide.
A canvas of silence, brushes drawn near,
Harmonies woven, each note crystal clear.

Violet sighs in the cool evening breeze,
Crimson echoes around the old trees.
Each stroke a heartbeat, alive in the night,
A symphony painted in vibrant light.

Shadowed corners hum secrets untold,
Bright visions of courage, vivid and bold.
With every hue, stories softly blend,
This opus of twilight will never end.

Listen closely to the pulse of the sky,
In colors that dance, watch the moments fly.
A masterpiece forming, one song at a time,
In the symphony of life, we all must climb.

Vibrant Fragments

Pieces of life, scattered like dust,
Glimmers of hope, in change we trust.
Each fragment a story, waiting to be found,
A mosaic of moments, where dreams abound.

In laughter and tears, colors unite,
Painting our paths in shadows and light.
Shattered illusions, yet beauty remains,
In these vibrant fragments, love never wanes.

A swirl of emotions, intense and true,
Each hue tells a tale, just waiting for you.
Connections unbroken, through trials we weave,
In the rich tapestry, we learn to believe.

Let the fragments shine, let them all glow,
In the art of our lives, we continue to grow.
With passion and zeal, we'll dance through the day,
In vibrant creations, we'll find our way.

Murmurs in Pastels

Softly they speak, the colors so faint,
Whispers of warmth from shadows they paint.
Delicate tones of lavender and cream,
In harmony's cradle, we cradle our dream.

Like secrets told in the hush of the dawn,
Pastels awaken, new hopes to spawn.
Gentle caresses of breezes that sigh,
Wrapped in the softness of a lullaby.

Each stroke a promise, tender and sweet,
In pastel gardens, our hearts find their beat.
Moments suspended in time's gentle grasp,
In murmurs of color, we lovingly clasp.

So let them flow, let our spirits ignite,
In the quiet of beauty, we find our light.
In whispers of pastels, we'll find our way,
Through the echoes of dawn, to a brand new day.

A Kaleidoscope of Feelings

Through the lens of the heart, colors spin fast,
Emotions collide, a bright vivid blast.
Each turn reveals wonders that shift and sway,
In a kaleidoscope dance, we find our way.

Joy sparkles bright like a sun-kissed day,
While sorrow will deepen the hues on display.
Anguish and laughter, they twine and weave,
In the tapestry rich, we learn to believe.

Moments of stillness, a whisper of hope,
In the swirl of our lives, together we cope.
Friendship and kindness like petals unfold,
In this vibrant mosaic, our stories told.

So look through the glass, let your mind take flight,
In this kaleidoscope bright, find your light.
For in every color, a feeling reveals,
The beauty of living, the depth that it steals.

Spectrum of Self

Colors collide in my mind,
Each hue a truth to find.
In shadows and light, I blend,
A journey that will not end.

Waves of blue on the shore,
Whispers of my heart's core.
Yellows bright with joy expressed,
A canvas of dreams, unpressed.

Greens of growth, a steady climb,
Rhythms dance in perfect rhyme.
Echoes of laughter, soft and clear,
In every shade, I hold dear.

Red for the passion that burns strong,
In every note, I sing my song.
Through the spectrum, I will weave,
A tapestry of me, believe.

Radiant Reflections

Mirrors of light dance and sway,
Holding fragments of the day.
In their glow, I start to see,
The hidden parts of me.

Ripples shimmer on the lake,
Every glance, a small heartache.
From the depths, I draw my voice,
In reflections, I rejoice.

Glimmers caught in morning dew,
Life's vibrant brush strokes, anew.
In the stillness, dreams take flight,
Carried softly by the night.

Infinite paths to explore,
Every shadow speaks of lore.
With each sparkle, I reclaim
The radiant essence of my name.

Chroma of Dreams

Whispers of color fill the air,
In this world, I lay bare.
Each dream a stroke, vivid and bright,
Painting the canvas of the night.

A twilight blend of purple skies,
Where hopes and wishes freely rise.
The golden rays of morning light,
Chase away the fears of night.

Strokes of orange with crimson threads,
Dancing through the thoughts in my head.
In every shade, a story told,
A vibrant script of dreams, bold.

A kaleidoscope of what could be,
In each vision, I am free.
With this chroma, I will soar,
Awakening dreams forevermore.

Prisms of My Spirit

Shattered light through crystal veins,
Pouring color, breaking chains.
In every shard, a piece of me,
Reflecting all I strive to be.

Soft echoes of laughter ring,
In the prisms, I take wing.
Vivid memories caught in time,
Each facet tells a tale in rhyme.

Through the spectrum, hearts entwine,
Every color, a sacred sign.
In the stillness, my truth glows,
Guided by where the spirit flows.

With every glance, I find my way,
In the light of a brand-new day.
The prisms shine with endless grace,
In the spectrum, I find my place.

Milton Keynes UK
Ingram Content Group UK Ltd.
UKHW021207261024
450281UK00007B/88